THE WORLD OF
CARL SANDBURG

THE

CARL

A Stage Presentation

New York

WORLD OF SANDBURG

by **NORMAN CORWIN**

HARCOURT, BRACE & WORLD, INC.

CONTENTS

Introduction vii

PART ONE   1

PART TWO   55

Appendixes

SANDBURG TRIBUTE AT U.C.L.A.   101

NOTES ON DIRECTION   103

NOTES   106

ORIGINAL "MACHINE" LINES   113

WHEN CARL SANDBURG and I were young men (he was sixty, I was twenty-eight), I did my first adaptation of his works, for broadcast over CBS. That was nearly a quarter of a century ago. As he did not disown the product, and in fact rather liked what he heard, I was encouraged to follow up, at respectable intervals of a few years, with a second, third and fourth program. One was a one-act opera, outfitted with a big orchestra, chorus, cast and the large presence of Burl Ives. Another was a "synthesis" of Sandburgiana starring Charles Laughton.

One day in the fall of 1958, Leonard Karzmar approached me with the request that I create a production honoring the poet, the proceeds of which were to go to a charity for which Karzmar was working. Now a large-scale tribute to Sandburg had long been the dream of many a Sandburg aficionado beside myself—notably Donna Workman, a Chicago business-woman of heart, energy and imagination. She had wanted to hold such an event in Soldiers' Field, which can accommodate 100,000 persons, and she had broached the subject to me a year earlier, but for logistical reasons, meaning committee gears that could not mesh, this dream was not realized.

So I said yes to Karzmar. The upshot was a star-filled evening in Royce Hall, on the campus of the University of California at Los Angeles. (Students and biographers of both Sandburg and Hollywood who may be interested in the cast and book of that production will find details in the Appendix.) The evening was a success by any standard, and everyone went home happy.

Months went by. The Sandburg Tribute—for such it was called—had been all but forgotten when one day Armand Deutsch and an associate, Judd Bernard, asked me whether I had any suggestions for an evening of "concert style" theater —a field they were about to enter. It took me a few minutes to think about Sandburg, for I had never associated commercial possibilities with the events of that evening. I played a tape recording of the Royce Hall tribute; they liked it and wanted to form a partnership. Sandburg consented; we entered a three-way agreement, and I proceeded to work up a script.

The World of Carl Sandburg had to be widely removed from that of the Tribute since no producer in the business, not even Todd at his palmiest, could have afforded the cast we gathered for Royce Hall. The concept, approach, progression, staging, lighting, interstices, all had to be different. What it had in common with the Royce Hall program was simply authorship, adaptorship and directorship.

I decided three persons would be enough to carry the weight earlier distributed among thirty at Westwood, providing the three had sufficient versatility. Deutsch and Bernard signed Bette Davis and her husband, Gary Merrill, to a contract—script unseen. Then I remembered a folk-singer I had heard years earlier in Richard Sanville's living room—Clark Allen. We engaged him to sing tunes from Sandburg's *Songbag*.

For the convenience of the Merrills, who lived on Cape Elizabeth outside Portland, the production moved to Maine. We rehearsed in an old Grange hall near Portland Head

Light. Whenever fog hung over the Cape, the foghorn of that lighthouse gave an abyssal obbligato to Sandburg's words, and, I am afraid, suggested the disruptive pun in the introduction to the "Fog" poem.

There were two previews in a theater on the campus of Bowdoin College, and we opened in Portland's biggest movie house—the State—on October 12, 1959. Sandburg flew up from his home in North Carolina for the opening. His visit carried almost the entire front page of the *Portland Press Herald*. Under three deep photographs of Sandburg that straddled eight columns, ran the legend, "The Face of America Shines on Portland."

After Portland the company went by road (its sole mode of travel) to Manchester, N. H.; Lowell, Mass.; and Hartford, New London, and Stratford, Conn. In none of these cities did it do well at the boxoffice. Press notices were excellent, but before they appeared in print we were off and away to the next city. To make matters grimmer, there was the incident of the New London date. A prominent elderly woman of the city had bought a seat in the first row, because—as she told friends on entering the theater—she had admired Bette Davis for many years, and at last was to see her in person. Five minutes before the opening curtain she slumped over, dead of a heart attack.

With a bleak first week behind, the sun broke through in Boston. Though the first unanimously enthusiastic press was not to come until a few days later in Philadelphia, the two performances at Symphony Hall were triumphant from the standpoint of audience reception. Fanfarades sounded in cities as far apart as Brooklyn, Atlanta, New Orleans, Hollywood, San Francisco. In only three cities on the road were critics disapproving. Elsewhere the press ranged from cordial to enraptured.

The original tour of 21 weeks ended at the Alcazar Theater in San Francisco on April 23, 1960. The following fall, on September 14, the show reopened at the Henry Miller Theater in New York City to cheers graphically described by Walter Kerr in the *Herald Tribune:* "Bette Davis found herself nearly blown through the back wall by the size of the ovation." For this production, Lief Erickson replaced Gary Merrill (the Merrills having separated in the interim). Erickson later said his personal notices were the best of his career.

Notwithstanding four out of seven favorable reviews for the show in the New York press, *The World of Carl Sandburg* lasted only a month on Broadway. Many convenient excuses were advanced: it ran into the Jewish holidays; Khrushchev, Tito, Castro, and the biggest brass of international diplomacy had descended on United Nations headquarters and the city was in a tizzy about them; the price scale was too high for this kind of show; it was unseasonably hot, cold, wet, etc., etc. The plain fact is that not enough New Yorkers came to see the show, which is one of the best reasons for a show to close. It had benefited from extraordinary publicity in all media; apparently it was just not Broadway fare. Others can rationalize and moralize about why shows which are hugged to the bosoms of big cities across the country are often given only polite nods, or less, in New York. Sandburg and I, in our separate ways, had other concerns, and we gladly left this sport to the experts.

So much for the history of the original production. As for the words and music:

Ten of Sandburg's published volumes are represented; eighteen items that had never seen print are here published in book form for the first time.

Sandburg, having been lulled by earlier adaptations I made of his writing, gave me his usual generous permission to make whatever abridgments I found necessary. As on those prior occasions, I was careful to do no knowing violence. Minor cuts within poems were made in a few instances, for a variety of reasons, the most fascinating of which were dictated by audience reactions. For example, in the moving poem, "Mildred Klinghofer," the uncut verse reads:

In her middle forties her first husband died.
In her middle sixties her second husband died.
In her middle seventies her third husband died,
And she died at mid-eighty with her fourth
  husband at her bedside.

It never occurs to the reader of the printed poem that there
is anything less than poignant in the synopsis of this life; but
theater audiences, undergoing that curious sea-change between reading something by one's self, and hearing it en
masse, was amused at the point where Mildred outlives her
third husband; there was some mild laughter, not unkind.
And although Miss Davis' performance was never affected by
it (both she and the poem being strong enough to ride over
a fleeting laugh where one does not belong), I nevertheless
yielded to the philosophy that anything, however minor,
which interrupts an emotional trajectory is best out of the
way. So I reduced the husbands by two. In this volume the
cut is restored.

In three instances minor additions were made. In "They
All Want to Play Hamlet," the quote from Hamlet's soliloquy
is not part of the Sandburg poem, but was inserted to animate
palely the tableau of Merrill and Yorick's skull.

In the passage concerning audiences which follows the
Hamlet piece, we wanted to accommodate the ever-present
coughers of all climes and seasons. Sandburg and I sat in a
hotel room the night before the opening, trying out phrases
that might tweak, yet not insult both coughers and their vic-
tims in the audience. Finally we settled on "Still others cough
as though they were ready for the coffin," and it went into
the show.

Sandburg himself added a line to "Joy." During the opening night's performance, he leaned over and whispered, "That
last line should be repeated." From then on, Miss Davis always said a second time, with a quietly stepped-up earnestness,
"Keep away from the little deaths."

Minor reiterations for the sake of rhythmic insistence, and an altered appearance on the page, were added to the "Machine" poem. And of course large cuts were made within the Lincoln passage that concluded the program. Outside of that, it was pristine Sandburg all the way, threaded together by my own commentary, which I used as sparingly as I could, and then only to give whatever orientation might be necessary for members of the audience who were not as familiar with the poet as his established fans. Even then, a few critics took exception to my writing *anything* in between.

As for the style of the "script" itself, it is here presented in substantially the form in which audiences saw it. But as this is unavoidably deficient in respect of dimensions such as fluid lighting, physical movement, special microphonic effects and the simple yet curiously warm-feeling set, we decided to abandon the strictly textual play form, and, by changing to past tense the stage business, have tried to convey a little more of the atmosphere. In other words, we tell the reader how it was, instead of prompting a stage company as to how it should be.

Merrill's place on the stage was taken by Barry Sullivan at one point in the tour, and by Erickson on Broadway, but for the purposes of this record, it makes sense, sentimentally and otherwise, to keep Gary Merrill in the starting lineup.

My narrative comments, written to link disparate elements and give shape and progression to the program, could not possibly do for the material what Sandburg himself could have done, had he gone on tour with the players. In preparing the manuscript for this book, I prevailed on Sandburg to say a few things about each selection. He did, in the form of a conversation between us that was stenographically preserved—quips, asides, and all. This dialogue appears on left-hand pages opposite the piece discussed. The play script, without interruption, runs continuously on right-hand pages.

Assigned to the appendix is a sheaf of notes toward interpretation of the poems for stage performance, which I wrote for Barry Sullivan when he took over Merrill's role on an emergency basis. As Sullivan was handicapped by inadequate time to rehearse, these notes served as homework, to help him overtake the handicap; which he certainly did. The notes are included here for readers who may care to try Sandburg out loud for themselves or anybody they can get to listen.

NORMAN CORWIN

Sherman Oaks, California
May 1, 1961

"Isn't that an iceberg on the horizon, Captain?"

"Yes, Madam."

"What if we get in a collision with it?"

*"The iceberg, Madam, will move right along
    as though nothing had happened."*

PART ONE

PART ONE

THE CURTAIN rose on a stage bathed in a warm, soft light. Across the back of the stage were spread folding screens of a neutral colored fabric framed in sturdy Salem maple, which served to draw the eye forward from the vastness of many of the outsized prosceniums into which the show was booked.

Before the screens stood four pieces of furniture which anticipated not only occupancy, but words and music. The centerpiece was a large, somewhat baroque throne-like chair on which rested a guitar and a dozen books. Even more books were piled at the foot of the chair; in effect it suggested an egghead's cornucopia. Flanking the throne chair downstage were three stools, spaced at even intervals across the stage.

The setting having been established, there emerged from the wings a man whose middling stature, deep-set eyes, strong nose and chin, and shock of straight hair heading downbrow toward the left ear, made him look a little like Sandburg himself before his locks went white. This was Gary Merrill.

He spoke:

MERRILL We're going to travel fast and far tonight because we have a world to girdle and cross in less than two hours: the fabulous world of Carl Sandburg, some of it hitherto unexplored.

We may be prejudiced, but we think Sandburg's world is as big as any man's that ever lived, and greater than most. But in any case, we hope you will share with us certain thrills of discovery. For one thing, some of the pieces you hear tonight have not yet been published, and Mr. Sandburg has given us the privilege of introducing them to the world, through you.

Having said this much, let it be known that my name is Gary Merrill and that there are three of us in the act here, including the first woman explorer ever to go out into space above Sandburg's world—Bette Davis. But before you meet her, meet some of the props: Since we are dealing with a poet, and metaphor is the soul of poetry, we use three obvious symbols to represent him. This chair is the one he would sit in if he were here; he would strum the guitar; and the books are what is published of his writing. Though none of us can fill his chair or do more than flick over the surface of his writings, it is entirely possible to engage his guitar, and for this purpose we have enlisted Clark Allen.

Allen entered, crossed over to Merrill, who handed him the guitar.

ALLEN Nowhere in the world is there such a boastful panorama of history as in a song called "I Was Born Almost Ten Thousand Years Ago." It's in The American Songbag, not on the basis of its simple-minded melody but because— to quote Mr. Sandburg—"it's a vest-pocket encyclopaedia that packs a wicked lot of biography."

Sandburg's full comment in the Songbag:

Folk lore tells of giants and long-lived men. On far travels they saw and heard much. . . . Also hoary legends have dealt with the Champion Liar. . . . We have in this instance a vest-pocket encyclopaedia, an outline of history with numerous references to picturesque personages. . . . It packs a wicked lot of biography.

For the show, only five of the original seven verses were used, and a parenthetical genealogical note added to the last verse.

I was born almost ten thousand years ago,
And there's nothing in the world that I don't know;
I saw Peter, Paul and Moses,
Playing ring-around-the-roses
And I'm here to lick the guy what says 'tain't so.

I saw Satan when he looked the garden o'er,
Saw Adam and Eve driven from the door,
And behind the bushes peeping,
Saw the apple they were eating,
And I'll swear that I'm the guy what ate the core.

I saw Samson when he laid the village cold,
Saw Daniel tame the lions in the hold,
And helped build the Tower of Babel,
Up as high as they were able,
And there's lots of other things I haven't told.

I taught Solomon his little A-B-C's,
I helped Brigham Young to make Limburger cheese,
And while sailing down the bay
With Methusaleh one day,
I saved his flowing whiskers from the breeze.

Queen Elizabeth she fell in love with me—
(Not the present Queen. . . . Elizabeth the First)
We were married in Milwaukee secretly,
But I schemed around and shook her,
And I went with General Hooker
To shoot mosquitos down in Tennessee.

CS: I started *Remembrance Rock* in 1943. The Prologue and first two books were written while the war was still on; Book 3 and the Epilogue came after the war. Five years in the writing— six hundred and seventy-three thousand words —1,057 pages!—all having to do with the American Dream and why this nation is a nation. Allan Nevins tells me he uses it in his classes in American history. Hugo Black sent me a wonderful letter about it; and I have a letter from a Captain of Marines in Norfolk, Va., telling me he read it three times.

The paragraph about the baby being God's opinion that life should go on, is part of a speech by Justice Windom to his granddaughter-in-law Mimah when she brings her infant—his great-grandson—into the library of his home for a visit.

NC: When did you first start to write for and about children?

CS: When my own children first started reading books.

On the basis of first things first, one logically starts with children—not those at the cowboy or Superman stage, but babies . . . infants. Sandburg has many things to say and ask about babies: "The sacred legion of the just-born . . . how many thousands born this minute?"

The answer is that there are about 200,000 babies born every day throughout the world. And to Sandburg, each is considerably more than a bundle that mewls and pukes in his nurse's arms. There is a paragraph in Sandburg's novel, Remembrance Rock, in which he has things to say about it.

A baby is God's opinion that life should go on. Never will a time come when the most marvelous recent invention is as marvelous as a newborn baby. The finest of our precision watches, the most supercolossal of our supercargo planes, don't compare with a newborn baby in the number and ingenuity of coils and springs, in the flow and change of chemical solutions, in timing devices and interrelated parts that are irreplaceable. A baby is very modern. Yet it is also the oldest of the ancients. A baby doesn't know he is a hoary and venerable antique—but he is. Before man learned how to make an alphabet, how to make a wheel, how to make a fire, he knew how to make a baby—with the great help of woman and his God and Maker.

There is a poem in The People, Yes, that collection of what he describes as "psalms, memoranda, sayings and yarns," in which Sandburg sounds a fanfare for the just-born. Since it's an ovation for Arrival, it has added fitness of giving an entrance to our star, who has several children of her own:
Ladies and gentlemen, Miss Bette Davis.

Miss Davis entered—(always to an ovation).

CS: As a boy I attended a series of performances
—admission free—of the Kickapoo Indians; I
tell about it in *Always the Young Strangers*.
They sold Sagwa, a tonic, that was supposed to
cure general lassitude. It competed with Hood's
and Ayer's Sarsaparilla. There was nothing in
what these Kickapoos did that was at all con-
nected with the noble Indian spirit of this poem.
When I wrote it I had been under the influence
of a translation of Indian songs and poems by
Frances Densmore, a woman who lived in Red
Wing, Minnesota, and who had been adopted
into several Indian tribes. Also around that
time I went through books of Indian lore, and
was struck by this legend in particular. It blesses
the helpless until they get their start.

Can you make baby poems
For those who love special babies—
        clean antiseptic babies?
what of those Red Indian babies
fresh from the birthing-crotch?
For each of them the mystery-man raised
his right hand toward the sky and called:
"Hey you sun moon stars
        and you winds clouds rain mist,
        "Listen to me! listen!
"The news is another baby belonging
        has come to this earth of ours.
"Make its path smooth so it can reach
        the top of the first hill
        and the second hill.
"And hey you valleys rivers lakes trees grasses
you make its path smooth so it can reach
        the top of the third hill.
        "And listen you birds of the air,
        you animals of the tall timbers,
        you bugs and creepers,
        you too listen!
"All you of sky earth and air, I ask you, beg you
"Pass this baby on till it climbs up over
        and beyond the fourth hill.
"From then on this child will be strong enough
"To travel on its own and see what is *beyond*
        those four hills!"

Beyond the four hills lie many worlds, including that of Carl
Sandburg. And a growing child can do much worse for himself
than to get lost in its byways and backwoods, for there is never
fright in being so lost—only fun and the glint of freshness.
    First there are the creatures. Like some of those borderline

CS: This is part of a series of imaginary anecdotes that are healthy for anybody's sanity. They pertain to a world somewhat like that of the *Rootabaga Stories*. But you might say they are in a different *métier*. This one in particular gives the back of the hand to impedimenta and vexations.

Sometimes, when I'm writing this kind of thing, I set up some paper on a typewriter, and when I start, it takes over and possesses me; and after a while I shake it off, and it no longer possesses me.

NC: Ever chuckle at one of your own lines?

CS: No, but I might feel good about it.

NC: Now about these Hoomadooms, Hongdorshes and Onkadonks . . . are they related, or do they live in discrete worlds?

CS: Oh, they know each other, in the way that the Slavs and Poles and Slovaks are different, but related.

Now that line about the frozen fish and the hot waffle—that'll go for thousands of editorials, and it also has the quality of a fable. On a challenge, it could go as a conversation between two characters.

Sometimes I've asked, "How do myths start?" I decided I would make a few myths, and get some distance out of them.

NC: Distance? What do you mean, distance?

CS: Well, isn't a myth as good as a mile?

NC: God!

CS: Never mind your pained reaction; you know you like it. You are an addict and still hooked.

NC: Back to the Hongdorshes, Carl.

CS: I did a page and a half of "Says and Ways Among the Hongdorshes," and some of them were a little too smart.

NC: How do you mean, a little too smart?

CS: I refuse to think up a specimen.

species between plant and animal life, Sandburg's creatures are of indeterminate sex, age, size and substance. They behave like human beings at times, and then again they don't. The Hoomadooms, for example: they make a big thing of Nothingness in an unpublished children's piece called "Brother Nothings."

SHE-HOOMADOOM   Suppose you have nothing to do till to-morrow, and tomorrow doesn't come?

HE-HOOMADOOM   (*thinking about it*) I wouldn't think about it; I wouldn't fold my thumb about it; I wouldn't beg my big toe to wiggle once about it; I would just do nothing till tomorrow didn't come.

SHE   Are you good at doing nothing?

HE   (*with mounting braggadocio*) I can do nothing better and more fancy, I can wrap up nothing faster, and tie nothing around it to *hold* it with nothing, faster than anybody else who ever had nothing, and knew how to *do* nothing *with* it.

All my life I do nothing nohow in no time for no pay and no be-sorry and no regrets and no respects. No tongues, no words, no long letters and no big box-car numbers, can tell how deep in nothings I get up in the morning, how far I fetch the fish in a *sea* of nothings, how always I have learned to expect nothing around the corner, so when I come to any other nothings like myself anywhere, they greet me, hold me, shake me, kiss me, as a brother nothing.

(*They kiss*)

There is a wise, more serious, less nothing-minded species than the Hoomadooms named the Hongdorshes, who lean toward speculation and the pursuit of knowledge. As usual, Sandburg is reticent about the physical appearance of his creatures; he gives us no inkling of what Hongdorshes look like, nor where to seek them, almost as though he were afraid that if we found them, we would quickly commercialize, contaminate and tax them. He does, however, tell us something about their habits:

When they speak what is so, they stand on the right foot; when they speak what is not so, they stand on the left foot; when they don't know what they are talking about, they stand fast on both feet and try to get their feet loose from the foot tracks. And it isn't as easy as you think.

It must have been a right-foot-speaking Hongdorsh who decided, after studying mankind, that there is a relationship between human knowledge and the flea.

The man who knows everything has fleas in each ear, and *they* look up the answers.

Now and then Hongdorshes are critical of each other. One of their sayings goes like this:

Put a price on the ocean and try to sell it. Some Hongdorsh will be sure to say, "I would buy it, only I already have three or four oceans at home."

The dreaming and wondering Hongdorsh, who we suspect may be Sandburg himself, asks profound questions:

Can there be a place so lonesome the moonlight runs away scared of it?

CS: I tried to make verbal music in this one. To some people it borders on the silly. In a certain sense, relaxation comes with the right kind of silliness.

Sandburg, in the Songbag:

A traditional lullaby in the City of Athens, State of Georgia, as written, words, air, and harmonization by Maybelle Stith of that city and state.

Lastly there is a Hongdorsh proverb, no doubt from some mighty Solomon among Hongdorshes:

Telling a frozen fish it is a hot waffle helps no more than telling a hot waffle it is a frozen fish.

Still in the pale of childhood, there is an unpublished Sandburg lullaby that magically combines beauty and nonsense.

Come to me dreaminess
come to me soon and see me
go sleep go slip go slag
come down oh dreaminess
come falling slow
come falling long and slow
now when the leaves are falling
now in the falltime moon
come springerly sprangerly sprong
come desta podesta dreaminess
now at the fall of leaves
now in the falltime moon

We asked Mr. Sandburg where he got the phrase "desta podesta," and he said it was the name of a girl he knew long ago; he thought it was musical enough to belong in a poem. Here's another lullaby—this one in song—from Sandburg's Songbag out of Athens, Georgia.

Go to sleepy, little baby,
'Fo' de booger man ketch you.
When you wake you'll have a piece of cake
And a whole lot of little horses.
Go to sleepy, little baby,
'Fo' de booger man ketch you.
When you wake you shall have a cake,

CS: If you get sufficiently vehement with kids about *not* doing something, the more you arouse their curiosity about how it would be if they did it. An old friend of mine in college told me about a safety pin that got caught in his baby's throat; but that is not as remarkable as an old doctor friend of mine—in his 60's—who did the same thing—got a safety pin caught in his throat.

NC: How and why?

CS: I haven't the faintest idea how it got there, and it's too late tonight to find out.

Coach and four little ponies,
A black and a bay, and a dapple and a gray.
Go to sleepy, little baby.

Beyond the lullaby stage, Sandburg knows all about growing children. A measure of that knowledge is contained in a little quickie of a poem from The People, Yes—phrased in the form of just two unanswered questions.

"Why did the children
put beans in their ears
when the one thing we told the children
they must not do
was put beans in their ears?"

"Why did the children
pour molasses on the cat
when the one thing we told the children
they must not do
was pour molasses on the cat?"

At the age of 77, Sandburg published the first volume of his autobiography, Always the Young Strangers.

In a chapter on his school days, he goes into the nicknames he heard around him when he was a kid. In no time, he evokes in every one of us associations and memories of our own school days—the sweetness and bitterness, the frivolity, the cruelty of children:

Once a ring of boys stood around a little fellow, calling him "Ah-ah." When I asked why, I was told, "He had to leave the room this morning, and he said to the teacher, 'I have to ah-ah.'"

There are nicknames that make a picture like a funny drawing. A girl was called "Squaremouth." Her mouth wasn't a funny nor an ugly mouth, and it wasn't actually square, but

it wasn't strictly round either . . . A boy would say, "Here comes Squaremouth." If it reached her, there was something about it that the boy could well be ashamed of.

One or two of the boys were called "Skinny" or "Fats" on account of that's what they were. A boy eleven years old was nicknamed "Fits" and they thought it smart to call him Fits. At recess in the schoolyard he might be walking around or standing still, when all of a sudden his head would be thrown back and his eyes turned up showing mostly the whites of the eyes. He just stood in his foot tracks and didn't see or hear anything going on around him. It was a spell, a sickness, though it didn't give him any pain. He would come out of it and be himself again. He was fair in his classes, kept quiet, went by himself, had a good face. The nearest I came to a fight in the schoolyard was one day when a fellow about my size blurted out, "Hello Fits" and I slapped him a stinger on the mouth. I didn't like his mouth.

The bell rang for us to go into the schoolrooms. He said he was going to fight it out with me. After school one day he put a chip on his shoulder and dared me to knock it off, which I did, and he didn't start fighting. Then I put the chip on my shoulder and he knocked it off, and I didn't start fighting. One way and another, we never did get to our fight.

I remember only one fight where I bloodied another boy's nose. What we fought about I can't remember. We were friends before and after the fight. His mother brought him to our house, showed my mother the bloody nose, and my mother said she would talk to me about it and see that it didn't happen again.—And it didn't.

In the literature of growing up, there are very few great examples of advice to the young. Polonius to Laertes in Hamlet, *Kipling's "If," and after that, you're on your own. But Polonius was a Lord Chamberlain speaking to a noble son; his*

CS: A long-time friend of mine in Chicago had a son aged 17, and already six feet high, handsome and bright; and he asked me, "What shall I tell my boy about how to live his life?" I wrote this for him. It's got a theory of education for parents to study.

NC: Did you ever get letters from parents telling you they found this poem useful?

CS: Yes.—By the way, did I show you the letter I got recently from a girl of 18 about the effect some of my stuff had on her?

NC: No.

After some search CS produced the letter which was postmarked "Hicksville, N. Y." It began:

Perhaps you may think me foolish for writing this, but I feel I have to, to thank you for your poetry.

The writer went on to explain that she was in the third year of high school; that a year ago she had been introduced to Sandburg's poetry, and that she had read it from time to time, and found in it always a sense of "greatness and peace." Then two final paragraphs:

Mr. Sandburg, mostly I want to thank you for my being alive today. A few months ago I reached the bottom of my life, or what I thought to be so at the time. The cause is irrelative: only the outcome is important. There were enough sleeping pills in the next room to kill me, but I could not get at them for a few hours. To pass the time

advice has a tint of blue in its veins: Kipling's "If" has almost too much red blood, considering lines like:

> *Yours is the Earth and everything that's in it,*
> *And—which is more—you'll be a Man, my son.*

But Sandburg's advice to a son nearing manhood could be from any father to any son. . . . It occurs in The People, Yes, *Section 9.*

A father sees a son nearing manhood.
What shall he tell that son?
"Life is hard; be steel; be a rock."
And this might stand him for the storms
and serve him for humdrum and monotony
and guide him amid sudden betrayals
and tighten him for slack moments.
"Life is a soft loam; be gentle; go easy."
And this too might serve him.
Brutes have been gentled where lashes failed.
The growth of a frail flower in a path up
has sometimes shattered and split a rock.
A tough will counts. So does desire.
So does a rich soft wanting.
Without rich wanting nothing arrives.
Tell him too much money has killed men
and left them dead years before burial:
the quest of lucre beyond a few easy needs
has twisted good enough men
sometimes into dry thwarted worms.
Tell him time as a stuff can be wasted.
Tell him to be a fool every so often
and to have no shame over having been a fool
yet learning something out of every folly
hoping to repeat none of the cheap follies
thus arriving at intimate understanding
of a world numbering many fools.
Tell him to be alone often and get at himself

until I could end it all, I sat down and read. Again, I found the same refuge I had found before. When I was able to take the pills, I no longer wished to. From words carefully arranged in patterns on paper I found a new hope—a will to go on. Today I realize I have a wonderful life ahead of me. I am engaged; one of the many mutual interests between my fiance and I (sic) is your poetry.

As I write this I hope so much that it will reach you. Again, with all my heart, soul and being, I thank you, Mr. Sandburg, for life, love, and peace.
With great respect and humility,

A very thankful young girl

CS: This was written when members of a graduating class in Crane High School, Chicago, wrote me collectively, asking me what to look out for in life.

and above all tell himself no lies about himself
whatever the white lies and protective fronts
he may use amongst other people.
Tell him solitude is creative if he is strong
and the final decisions are made in silent rooms.
Tell him to be different from other people
if it comes natural and easy being different.
Let him have lazy days seeking his deeper motives.
Let him seek deep for where he is a born natural.
    Then he may understand Shakespeare
    and the Wright brothers, Pasteur, Pavlov,
    Michael Faraday and free imaginations
bringing changes into a world resenting change.
        He will be lonely enough
        to have time for the work
        he knows as his own.

For sons who have already grown up, and have sons of their own, Sandburg has some other advice: It is contained in an unpublished cautionary poem called "Bewares":

Beware of respectable people,
    of people perfectly grammatical and proud of it,
    of crooks who mistake their crookedness for something else,
    of persons who let their thinking be done for them and
        don't know what is happening to them,
Beware of snobs as more pathetic than thieves, gamblers, con
        men,
Beware of those who laugh at original work not knowing all
        original work is laughed at to begin with,
Beware of yourself when forgetting how to use silence,
    of yourself when afraid of your deeper dreams,
Beware of yourself more than anybody else.
Beware when you fail to remember that man's fate on the
        earth
    is concentrated in the word: Struggle!

CS: The Mildred of this poem was an actual person, with a name close to Klinghofer, but not quite as musical. She was a neighbor in Maywood, Illinois. I knew her third husband very well. Charles Hanson Towne, in reviewing *The People, Yes,* said, "Every once in a while there's a novel in a single poem." This is one of them.

Sandburg himself has never forgotten that word. His own struggles have taken him through the crazily varied occupations of tinsmith, waiter, milk-wagon driver, wheat harvester, dishwasher, stoker, soldier, hobo, reporter, critic, novelist, historian, biographer. His life has spanned booms, depressions and five shooting wars; his journey has taken him from the age of the horse-drawn streetcar to the interplanetary missile. Throughout all this time, he has never forgotten his lowly beginnings, never upstaged the humble, never lost that pity which is akin to love, for fellow strugglers met with on the way. He has written about them scores of times—here are a few out of the hundreds—An old woman, two angry men, a married couple, and a rueful lover.

First, Mildred Klinghofer.

Mildred Klinghofer whirled through youth in bloom.
One baby came and was taken away, another came and was
    taken away.
From her windows she saw the cornrows young and green
And later the final stand at the corn and the huddled shocks
And the blue mist of a winter thaw deepening at evening.
In her middle forties her first husband died.
In her middle sixties her second husband died.
In her middle seventies her third husband died.
And she died at mid-eighty with her fourth husband at the
    bedside.
Thus she had known an editor, a lawyer, a grocer, a retired
    farmer.
To the first of them she had borne two children she had
    hungered for.
And deep in her had stayed a child hunger.
In the last hours when her mind wandered, she cried imperi-
    ously,
  "My baby! Give me my baby!"
And her cries for this child, born of her mind, in her final
   · moments of life, went on and on.

CS: Thomas Hornsby Ferril of Denver told me of the incident of this duel:

CS: I'm surprised that I don't hear about this piece being used by lawyers in proceedings for divorce. It has the gist of a hundred thousand divorces. John Milton didn't say much more in his long essay favoring divorce.

When they answered, "Your baby isn't here" or "Your baby
      is coming soon if you will wait," she kept on with her
      cry,
   "My baby! let me hold my baby!"
      And they made a rag doll
      And laid it in her arms
And she clutched it as a mother would.
And she was satisfied and her second childhood ended like
      her first, with a doll in her arms.

   There are dreams stronger than death.
   Men and women die holding these dreams.

      (*Note: In the show, there was no introductory material for
      the following three poems.*)

   In a Colorado graveyard
   two men lie in one grave.
They shot it out in a jam over who owned
One corner lot: over a piece of real estate,
They shot it out: it was a perfect duel.
Each cleansed the world of the other.
Each horizontal in an identical grave
Had his bones cleaned by the same maggots.
They sleep now as two accommodating neighbors.
They had speed and no control.
They wanted to go and didn't know where.

The law says you and I belong to each other, George.
The law says you are mine and I am yours, George.
And there are a million miles of white snowstorms, a million
      furnaces of hell,
Between the chair where you sit and the chair where I sit.
The law says two strangers shall eat breakfast together after
      nights on the horn of an Arctic moon.

Sandburg in the Songbag:

This poem, trying to ease heartbreak, uses the simplest of words. They go to a soft, brave melody. Its lyric cry is brief, poignant as Sappho. Its measures are close to silence and to art "to be overheard rather than heard."

CS: I had finished my morning work on the *Chicago Day Book*—an adless daily that was the darling of E. W. Scripps and ran from 1912 to 1917—and I had just gone down to the Loop to interview a juvenile court judge. On my way I branched off to Grant Park, and saw a fog over Chicago harbor. It was one of many fogs I had seen in my time, of course. Well, I had to wait forty minutes for my interview with the judge, and I took out my trusty lead pencil, and

Love, oh love, oh careless love,
Love, oh love, oh careless love,
It's love, oh love, oh careless love.
You see what love has done for me.

Sorrow, sorrow, to my heart,
When me and my true love have to part.
It's love, oh love, oh careless love.
You see what love has done for me.

Ain't it enough to break my heart,
To see my man with another sweetheart.
It's love, oh love, oh careless love.
You see what love has done for me.

Now my money's spent and gone,
You passed my door, a-singin' a song.
It's love, oh love, oh careless love.
You see what love has done for me.

I cried last night, and the night before,
Going to cry tonight, and I'll cry no more.
It's love, oh love, oh careless love.
You see what love has done for me.

You've gone and broke this heart of mine,
Going to break that heart of yours sometime,
It's love, oh love, oh careless love
You see what love has done for me.

There is a wisp of a poem about a fog that Sandburg never reads in public any more because he suspects its fabulous popularity. But we're going to do it because we feel fog would be missed on this program.

Though we are not going to be so rash as to use the sound effect of a foghorn to conclude the poem—(we certainly don't want any foghorn conclusions)—there is a bit of atmosphere that goes along with this piece.

on a piece of newsprint I wrote it while waiting
in some kind of anteroom.

Fact is, I had been carrying a pocketful of
Japanese Hokus. A hoku is where you have to
have exactly 17 syllables. If you have 16,
you're one short; 18, you have one too many.
It's far simpler than a sonnet. Well, I tried a free-
going, independent American Hoku.

NC: What, are there just 17 words in "Fog"?

CS: I don't know how many there are. The
piece has been set to music by six different com-
posers. The only one I can recall is Roy Harris.

NC: I guess that's your best known poem, isn't
it?

CS: That, and "Chicago." I did a Chicago poem
called "The Windy City"—far better in gathering that city. I was influenced by Indian poems
while writing "Chicago." I wrote it in the office
of "System," a business magazine, in 1913. I
was an associate editor.

NC: What was a lousy businessman like you
doing as associate editor of a business magazine?

CS: I submitted two articles, one entitled
"Muzzling the Machines," which had to do
with mechanical safeguards. It had a wonderful
photograph of a workman holding up a pair
of glasses, one lens of which had been shattered
by a steel splinter that would have blinded him
in that eye if it had not been for the glass.
He had a gorgeous grin on his face. That was
when workmen's compensation laws were being
passed by state legislatures—with Wisconsin,
under La Follette, taking the lead.

The other article was entitled "Training
Workers to be Careful."

Basically the poem is a chant of defiance by
Chicago . . . its defiance of New York, Boston,
Philadelphia, London, Paris, Berlin and Rome.
The poem sort of says "maybe we ain't got
culture, but we're eatin' regular."

The fog comes
on little cat feet.

It sits looking
over harbor and city
on silent haunches
and then moves on.

No poem is too small to be big; no people too big or little for
Sandburg's notice; neither are there any objects too large or
too inconspicuous. There have been many poets who have
looked at the world through rose-colored glasses, or through a
glass darkly, or through the glass of fashion, but God knows
what prescription went into the lens through which Sandburg
sees. He sees fun and color in objects we use every day without
thinking twice or even once about them—he sees stories in
them, fables, parables, and high nonsense.

GLASS. . . .
Glass is where your eye looks through and you
put your hand out and the glass stops it.

Looking glass is where you wonder where your
face came from.

Looking glass tells you how you think you look
when other people look at you.

Eye glasses are to take off when you are going
to fight with fists.

TABLE CLOTHS . . .
Table cloths never satisfy the tables.
Tables say table cloths are either too clean or too dirty.
Table cloths hate soup, coffee and gravy.
On a fresh table cloth the first spot of soup is the worst.
On a new table cloth two coffee spots look like ten.
On a spick and span table cloth a big gravy spot feels
    important.

NC: Do you still feel the same way about Chicago as when you wrote it?

CS: I will have a certain deep affection for Chicago as long as I live.

NC: Is there a runner-up in your affections, among American cities?

CS: Well, Milwaukee is the best governed large city in this country. That began when the Socialists elected a mayor.

NC: No, I meant physically.

CS: I'd say Chicago, New York, San Francisco. —Haven't we gotten away from "Fog" somewhat?

NC: Why not?

CS: Well, anyway, the fog was in Chicago.

CS: These are more of the Sanity pieces. Something childish, yet universal about them. There are times when the childish is basically wise.

SNAKES. . . .

Some snakes are all neck.
Girl snakes show off their curves.
Water snakes like water.
Moccasin snakes like moccasins.

BUGS . . .

When bugs come home they come home to bug houses.
When bugs meet they talk bug talk.
Ungrammatical bugs say, "How *is* things?"
Sixteen legged bugs sometimes lose a leg or two and don't
    notice it.
The shorter a short bug is, the more he brags how short he is.
The longer a long bug is, the more he hopes he will not break
    in the middle and be two short bugs.

NEWSPAPERS . . .

Newspapers are to start a fire with, if you have the wood.
Newspapers are to wrap up with and then unwrap.
Newspapers are to sit on at a picnic.
Newspapers are terrible when terrible things happen.
Newspapers tell beforehand what is going to happen—maybe.
Newspapers are to throw away today and wait till tomorrow
    comes.

FINGERS . . .

Each finger has its secrets.
The pointing finger is best at pointing.
Crook one finger and all the other fingers want to crook.
Bend one finger back and all the other fingers watch what
    happens.
Sometimes the fingers feel sorry the thumb is not a finger.

Look close at your thumb and you see it is not proud.

The fingers have two knuckles, a thumb only one knuckle,
    and they need each other.

As you have probably assumed by now, there is nothing sterile about Sandburg. He leaves obscurantism to the aesthetes; he gives wide berth to the labyrinth school which considers it treason to be understood. He never fusses with the passions in a test tube, never dissects and analyzes thought and emotion but deals with them frontally, fully. Here's a fragment called "Snatch of Sliphorn Jazz."

Are you happy? It's the only
way to be, kid.
Yes, be happy, it's a good nice
way to be.
But not happy-happy, kid, don't
be too doubled-up doggone happy.
It's the doubled-up doggone happy-
happy people . . . bust hard . . . they
do bust hard . . . when they bust.
Be happy kid, go to it, but not too
doggone happy.

Here is another short piece called "Joy." Its last line is particularly memorable and contains a suggestion by which its author has had no trouble living.

Let a joy keep you.
Reach out your hands
And take it when it runs by,
As the Apache dancer
Clutches his woman.
I have seen them
Live long and laugh loud,
Sent on singing, singing,
Smashed to the heart
Under the ribs
With a terrible love.

CS: There *are* people who manage to keep
away from the little deaths. Some of them live
long and some don't, but when they die, they
are not little deaths.

Joy always,
Joy everywhere—
Let joy kill you!
Keep away from the little deaths.

Sandburg does not believe all people necessarily have lights coming out of them. In fact, he has a great capacity to hate what is crass and ugly: snobs, bullies, dictators, phonies. He knows the workings of hate. . . .

If you hate a man let him live.
You may live to see him suffer.
He may live to see you suffer.
Or in the slow sliding away of days
you might both forget each other.

If you hate a man and you kill him
he will forget you and haunt you
unless you are poor at remembering.

If you hate a man and he kills you
at the same time you kill him
then the score is nothing to nothing.

When death comes,
one little room can hold
the big dome of the sky
and the ocean looks easy to wade in.

The obverse of hate is love. Thanks to its unending and deserved popularity, love has been the principal theme in every form of writing, from dirty limericks to Romeo and Juliet. Here are some Sandburg variations on themes of love, all sharing the distinction of being not yet published. The first is called "Be Proud If You Want To."

CS: I remember as a kid, having this feeling about a very lovely girl. I tell about it in *Always the Young Strangers*. What a time I had!

Tell me you love me.
I want to hear that come from you.
Lie if you must, say it as half the truth.
Say it to play me along.
I'd rather you'd two-time me than throw me over.
Say it like something not to be meant.
Only tell it to me once: say you love me.

Be proud if you want to.
Be proud about your looks, the house you live in
And the high education your mother had
and the way she brought you up right.
You'll see there won't be a whimper out of me.
Be proud, but say it for me once.
Say it like a good actress.
Say you'd like to have me around.

(At this, Miss Davis touched his cheek patronizingly with the nail buffer, rose from the chair, and came downstage to comment):

That one begs for an answer, but Sandburg is silent; it's as far as he goes.

(Merrill, after brooding about this for a moment at the now empty chair, shook it off and returned to circulation, at his stool of Salem maple.)

Sandburg in the Songbag:

Sympathy for the First Man is here . . .
College girls sing it. . . . Text and tune are
from the State Teachers College at Harrisonburg,
Virginia.

Among the varieties of love upon which Sandburg has mused is Mother-Love—at best, it's incorruptible; at worst, it gives us Mothers-in-Law. There's a song on the terrible effects of having no mother to love you, which amused Sandburg enough to bag it for his Songbag. . . . It's named "Old Adam" (Adam as of the Bible), who was an orphan before he was born. . . .

(Note: for the show, a new tune was written by NC when Allen protested that the original tune would not yield to his style of arrangement.)

I'm so sorry for old Adam,
 Just as sorry as can be;
For he never had no mammy
 For to hold him on her knee.

For he never had no childhood,
 Playin' round the cabin door,
And he never had no daddy
 For to tell him all he knoor.*

And I've always had the feelin'
 He'd a let that apple be,
If he'd only had a mammy
 For to hold him on her knee.

* ("Knew" in the original. NC took the liberty of altering it to rhyme with "door" although he knoor perfectly well there would be objections.)

CS: It came across me that all of the formidable characters in history had mothers, and that in most cases very little is known about them. Napoleon was a good-looking child, and his mother must have thought him a pretty sweet bundle. Did you know Napoleon was second to Jesus in the number of biographies written about him, until old Abraham Lincoln came along?

At the other end of the world from this impudent little song is Sandburg's poem on the subject of mothers: "Out of Windows Look Mother Faces."

The shadowy woman of hope
who bore Judas Iscariot—
could it be she leaned
at a window sill in the sun
refusing to believe beforehand
what came after?

Or the mother of J. Wilkes Booth
gazing at a child come well-made,
did a fear smite her early
with a gong she could never still?

And the black-eyed Corsican woman
who named her new baby Napoleon,
did she smile at the sweet bundle
and chat with neighbor women
telling them "He will be heard from"?

Out of windows look mother faces
knowing love is a deep well
and a mirror of shadow-changes:
here looms water for a deep thirst,
here gleams a looking-glass too dark
to print a face and foretell a fate
and bring a moan. . . .
"It can't be . . . I wouldn't have
believed it . . ."

Nancy Hanks at Rock Spring Farm
on the Big South Fork of Nolin's Creek,
how could she know
what the granny woman helped bring from her,
daybreak twilight of one February twelve,
she in a one-room house, a one-window cabin,
on leather hinges one door to a wide world?

CS: I wrote this originally for Marintha Wilming in *Remembrance Rock*. At the time, I knew it was getting too long for its place in the novel, but I couldn't stop when I got rolling. It's a variation on Cyrano—this gal was a kind of woman Cyrano.

The speech, as used in the show, reconciled a couple in Nashville that was drifting apart. I had a request for the text after the show played in Nashville; seems their engagement was about to be broken; after the text went off in the mail, I got notice of a wedding date.

Attila the Hun, he had a mother.
Shicklgruber too had a mother.
Michelangelo and J. Sebastian Bach,
each sucked strength at a mother breast—
and not one of the mothers held beforehand
sure foretokenings of what was to come:

they washed their babies smooth,
clean behind the ears, clean all over,
slippery gleaming to hands and eyes,
to the mothers fond and guessing,
to the mothers hoping and praying.

Out of windows look mother faces
knowing love is a deep well
and a mirror of shadow changes.

*To seal off PART I, Miss Davis brings us a rare jewel from
the Sandburg collection. It is a meditation on the forms of
love, and belongs high up, if not at the top, of uniqueness in
the language of love.*

> *(Merrill and Allen left the stage to Miss Davis for this
> soliloquy.)*

Love, is it a cat with claws and wild mate screams in the black
    night?
Love, l-o-v-e, is it a tug at the heart that comes high and costs,
    always costs, as long as you have it?
Love, is it a free glad spender, ready to spend to the limit and
    then go head over heels in debt?
Love, can it hit one without hitting two, and leave the one
    lost and groping?
Love, I said love, l-o-v-e, can you pick it up like a mouse and
    put it in your pocket and take it to your room and bring
    it out of your pocket and say, "Oh here is my love, my
    little pretty mousey love"?

Yes, love, this little word you hear about; is love an elephant and you step out of the way where the elephant comes trampling, tromping, traveling with big feet and long flaps of drooping ears and ivory tusks, and you step out of the way with respect, with *high* respect and a surprise near to a shock as you say, *"Jesus, he's big!"* Big like stupendous is big, heavy and elephantine and funny, immense and slow and easy, big like supercolossal is terrible and big—I'm asking, is love an elephant?

Or a snake, say like a rattlesnake, like a creeping winding slithering rattlesnake with fangs, poison fangs they tell me, and when the bite of it gets you, then you run crying for help if you don't fall cold and dead on the way—can love be a snake?

Or would you say love is a flamingo, with pink feathers, a soft sunset pink, a sweet gleaming naked pink, with enough long feathers you could make the fan for a fan-dance and hear a girl telling her lover, "Speak, my chosen one, and tell me what manner of fan dance you would have with me in the black velvet sheen of mid-night—" —could it be love is a flamingo?

Or could it be love is a big red apple and you don't know whether to bite into it, and you knock on wood and call off your luck numbers and hold your breath and put your teeth into it and get a mouthful of it and taste all there is to it; and whether it's sweet and wild or a dry mush you want to spit out, it's something else than you expected—I'm asking, kind sir, is love a big red apple?

Maybe it's goofer dust, I hadn't thought about that, for you go to the goofer tree at midnight and gather the leaves and crush them into fine dust, very fine, sir, and when your man sleeps you sprinkle it in his shoes, and he's helpless, and from then on he can't get away from you, for he's snared and tangled and can't keep from loving you—could goofer dust be the answer?

And are they after beguiling and befoozling us when they tell us love is a rose, a red, red rose, the mystery of leaves folded over and under, and you can take it to pieces and throw it away petal by petal into the wind, blowing it away, or you can wear it for a soft spot of crimson in your hair, at your breast, in a corsage, in a girdle, and you can waltz and rhumba wearing your sweet crimson rose, and take it home and lay it on a window sill in the sun and see it wither brown and curl black and shrivel to one day you're not careful, and it crackles into dust in your hand, and the wind whisks it whither you know not, whither you care not, whither you don't give one little solitary damn where it's gone, for it was just one more flame of a rose that came with its red blush and crimson bloom and did the best it could with what it had, and nobody wins, nobody loses, and what's one more rose? And on any street corner on bright summer mornings you see them with bunches of roses and their hands out toward you. . . . "Roses today, fresh roses from the bush . . . A rose for you, sir, the ladies like roses." . . .

Then there are those who say, "Love is a little white bird and the flight of it so fast you can't see it, and you know it's there only by the faint whirr of its wings and the hush song it sings. You listen keen and you listen long, and you'd like to write it but it can't be written, and you'd like to sing it but you don't dare try because the little white bird sings it better than you can; so you listen; and while you pray, and after you pray, you meditate, and then pray some more; and one day it's as though a great slow wind had washed you clean and strong inside and out, and the little white bird's hush-song telling you nothing can harm you; the days to come can weave in and weave out and spin their fabrics and designs for you, and nothing can harm you, unless you change yourself into a thing of harm, nothing can harm you—

The little white bird is my CANDIDATE, ladies and gentlemen! I give you the little white bird you can't see though you

can hear its hush song, and when you hear that hush song, it's *love*; and I'm ready to *swear* to it and you can bring in a stack of affidavits and I'll swear to it and sign my name to every last "So help me God," and if a fat bumbling shop-worn court clerk tells me, "Hold up your hand," I'll hold up my hand all right, and when he bumbles and mumbles to me like I was one more witness it was work for him to give the oath to, when he blabs, "You do solemnly swear that in this cause you will tell the truth, the whole truth and nothing but the truth," I'll say to him, "I *do*—and no thanks to you—and you could be more immaculate with the name of God!"

And so, I give you the little white bird—and my thanks for your hearing me—and my prayers for you—my deep, silent prayers.

(*This ended Part I.*)

PART TWO

BEFORE THE house lights dimmed all the way out, the voice of Allen was heard from behind the curtain, which rose on an empty set. After a moment Allen emerged from behind one of the screens and crossed to his stool, singing "John Henry" all the while with a driving energy unrelated to the pace of his physical movement. Midway in the song, Merrill emerged unobtrusively from the other side of the stage and occupied his stool. Then Miss Davis came out just as quietly as the other two— although the gown Orry Kelly had designed for her second act was not the kind that goes unnoticed. (In Hollywood, where wardrobe is a major arm of the film industry, Miss Davis' entrance at this point in the opening night's performance created a pandemonium second only to the three-minute ovation that greeted her first entrance.) The dress was of blue satin, with a wide red panel in the back. Diagonally across the front was a thin piping of red and white, like an extrapolated baldric. Long white gloves finished it off. Mr. Kelly said he designed his gown around the primary colors that he felt vibrating always in Sandburg's poems. After the stir of Miss Davis' return, Allen forged ahead with the steel-drivin' Mr. Henry.

Sandburg in the Songbag:

In the southern work camp gangs,
John Henry is the strong man, or the
ridiculous man, or anyhow the man
worth talking about, having a myth
character somewhat like that of
Paul Bunyan in work gangs of the
Big Woods of the North. He is related
to John Hardy, as balladry goes,
but wears brighter bandannas. . . .

CS: I told Tom Maloney, editor of *U. S.*
Camera, that "Phizzog" had never been run
in any photographic magazine. So he ran it. With
my phizzog as done by Steichen.

Now the captain said to John Henry,
"Gonna bring my steam-drill around."
"Well," John Henry said, "I'd rather be dead
Than let a steam-drill beat me down, Lord, God,
Than let a steam-drill beat me down. . . ."

Now John Henry said to that captain,
"Well, a man ain't nothin' but a man
And before I'd let that steam-drill beat me down
I'd die with a hammer in my hand, Lord, God,
I'd die with a hammer in my hand. . . ."

Well, John Henry was hammering at that mountain.
His hammer was strikin' fire.
He hammered so hard that he broke his poor back.
He laid down his hammer and he died, Lord, God,
He laid down his hammer and he died. . . .

Well, they took John Henry from that mountain,
Buried him down in the sand.
And every locomotive comes roarin' by
Says, "there lies a steel-drivin' man, Lord, God,
There lies a steel-drivin' man. . . ."

Sandburg reveals himself in a thousand ways, sometimes in the smallest fragments. . . . One of his most famous pieces is a poem so short you could wrap a cigarette in it. It's called "Phizzog."

This face you got,
This here phizzog you carry around,
You never picked it out for yourself,
    at all, at all—did you?
This here phizzog—somebody handed it
    to you—am I right?

CS: Across the 20's, I heard all the orchestras that were originating jazz; I'll take some of the pieces out of that period, like "Livery Stable Blues," as against the general run of jazz pieces today.

NC: How do you feel about swing, and rock and roll?

Somebody said, "Here's yours, now go see
   what you can do with it."
Somebody slipped it to you and it was like
   a package marked:
"No goods exchanged after being taken away"—
This face you got.

One of Mr. Sandburg's poems, written 50 years ago, proclaims his love for Nature, for the Arts, for history, for children, and for love itself. It ends with these lines:

   "If I live to a majestic old age, becoming the owner of a
      farm,
   I shall sit under apple trees in the summer and on a pad of
   paper with a large yellow lead pencil I shall write of these
   things, lover of mine . . ."

Well, the wonderful thing is that he has lived to a majestic old age; he has become the owner of a farm; he does sit under trees (maybe not apple trees, but trees) and he does write with a lead pencil on a pad of paper. A lively interest in all the arts flows from the tip of that lead pencil. Throughout his writings, you find Sandburg musing not only on man, on the forms and substances of nature, but on sculpture and painting, architecture and music, Bach and Brancusi. His musical awareness is represented by titles that are often little poems in themselves: "Four Preludes on Playthings of the Wind"; "Study in Fugue"; "Song for Indiana Ophelias"; "Consolation Sonata"; "Cadenza"; "Jazz Fantasia." The last of these evokes a whole age just as surely as the jazz of the jazz-men it celebrates. . . .

Drum on your drums, batter on your banjoes,
sob on the long cool winding saxophones.
Go to it, O jazzmen.

Sling your knuckles on the bottoms of the happy

CS: Each of them is a little sick.

NC: Presley?

CS: He's installed right over my office there at
20th Century-Fox. I met him; he was baffled.
I said, "I just want to shake your hand, so I can
tell people, 'Shake the hand that shook the hand
of Elvis Presley.' "

CS: This came out of my long association with
drama. I have quite a chapter on it in *Always
the Young Strangers.*

tin pans, let your trombones ooze, and go husha-
husha-hush with the slippery sand-paper.

Moan like an autumn wind high in the lonesome treetops,
    moan
soft like you wanted somebody terrible, cry like a racing
car slipping away from a motorcycle cop, bang-bang! you
jazzmen, bang altogether drums, traps, banjoes, horns,
tin cans—make two people fight on the top of a stairway
and scratch each other's eyes in a clinch tumbling down the
stairs.

Can the rough stuff . . . now a Mississippi steamboat pushes
up the night river with a hoo-hoo-hoo-oo . . . and the green
lanterns calling to the high soft stars . . . a red moon
rides on the humps of the low river hills . . . go to it,
O jazzmen.

*Though Sandburg has never attempted dramatic forms, he is
a favorite poet of actors. His subjects are often vivid and dramatic, his writing is meant to be spoken, and every now and
then he shows an amused, good-natured sympathy with the
acting craft. This comes through delightfully in "They All
Want to Play Hamlet."*

> *(After the introduction, Merrill moved up to the throne-
> chair, wrapped himself in a black cloak, and went into a
> Rodinesque pose with a skull in his extended left hand, and
> his chin pensively in his right. He was the Hamlet of the
> churchyard scene. Miss Davis stood to one side and indicated
> him as she would an exhibit.)*

They all want to play Hamlet.
They have not exactly seen their fathers killed
Nor their mothers in a frame-up to kill,
Nor an Ophelia dying with dust gagging the heart,
Not exactly the spinning circles of singing golden spiders,
Not exactly this have they got at nor the meaning of flowers—

CS: These are mostly proverbs about audiences, some of them quite old.

O flowers, flowers slung by a dancing girl—in the saddest
play the inkfish, Shakespeare, ever wrote;
Yet they all want to play Hamlet because it is sad like all
actors are sad and to stand by an open grave with a joker's
skull in the hand and then to say over slow and say over
slow wise, keen, beautiful words masking a heart that's
breaking, breaking . . .

HAMLET *Alas! Poor Yorick. I knew him, Horatio. . . .
A man of infinite jest and most excellent fancy. He hath
borne me on his back a thousand times. . . .*

This is something that calls and calls to their blood.
They are acting when they talk about it and they know it is
acting to be particular about it and yet: They all want
to play Hamlet.

*Sandburg has observed not only actors, but their audiences.
Here is a brief index of them:*

One audience may wheeze like a calliope with sore tonsils
and another roar like a burning lumber yard.

Some of them, as you look closer, are slow as molasses in
January—or quick as greased lightning.

Some are noisy as a cook-stove falling downstairs, and others
quiet as an eel swimming in oil.

Still others cough, as if ready for the coffin.

*Numbers have always had a powerful attraction for Sandburg,
both on and off the printed page. In "Arithmetic," he strikes
resonances that are only an octave above or below God's
truth.*

CS: Very small kids enjoy this poem, along with their elders. Also teachers like it.

NC: At the same time, it seems to me sophisticated from a scientific point of view. Have you heard from scientists about it?

CS: Yes. Some have asked me for permission to print it here and there in scientific journals. I wrote a poem once for IBM's *Think* Magazine, entitled "Micrometric Mirrors."

CS: This first ran in *The Nation*. I had letters from precisionists around the question, "What

Arithmetic is where numbers fly like pigeons in and out of your head.

Arithmetic tells you how many you lose or win if you know how many you had before you lost or won.

Arithmetic is seven eleven all good children go to heaven— or five six bundle of sticks.

Arithmetic is numbers you squeeze from your head to your hand to your pencil to your paper till you get the answer.

Arithmetic is where the answer is right and everything is nice and you can look out of the window and see the blue sky—or the answer is wrong and you have to start all over and try again and see how it comes out this time.

If you take a number and double it and double it again and then double it a few more times, the number gets bigger and bigger and goes higher and higher and only arithmetic can tell you what the number is when you decide to quit doubling.

Arithmetic is where you have to multiply—and you carry the multiplication table in your head and hope you won't lose it.

If you have two animal crackers, one good and one bad, and you eat one and a striped zebra with streaks all over him eats the other, how many animal crackers will you have if somebody offers you five six seven and you say No no no and you say Nay nay nay and you say Nix nix nix?

If you ask your mother for one fried egg for breakfast and she gives you two fried eggs and you eat both of them, who is better in arithmetic, you or your mother?

"The sea and the stars," says Sandburg, "are made and held by numbers." This quote may be a clue—perhaps the only clue—to one of his most mystical poems—"Monkey of Stars."

There was a tree of stars sprang up on a vertical panel of the south.

could it possibly mean?" I told them it means
whatever you'd like it to mean; and if you can't
have fun with it, I'm sorry.

And a monkey of stars climbed up and down in this tree
of stars.
And a monkey picked stars and put them in his mouth, tall
up in a tree of stars shining in a south sky panel.
I saw this and I saw what it meant and what it means was
five, six, seven, that's all, five, six, seven.
Oh hoh, yah yah, loo loo, the meaning was five, six, seven,
five, six, seven.

Panels of changing stars, sashes of vapor, silver tails of meteor
streams, washes and rockets of fire—
It was only a dream, oh hoh, yah yah, loo loo, only a dream,
five, six, seven, five, six, seven.

*It could be there is a faint echo of a Texan lullaby in that
poem, a lullaby called "By'M By," which is described by
Sandburg in his Songbag as referring to the "stealth and mystery of the coming out of the stars one by one on the night
sky . . ."*

By'm by, by'm by,
Stahs shinin',
Numbah, numbah one,
Numbah two, numbah three,
Good Lawd, by'm by, by'm by,
Good Lawd, by'm by.

*The same man who wrote about 5, 6, 7 and the fog coming
on little cat feet, has written the massive Lincoln biography.
That work would be enough to satisfy the historical yen of
most poets; but for Sandburg, dust never settles on the past.
Is six thousand years long in the chronicles of man? Not ac-
cording to the poem "Bilbea," whose subtitle explains that
it's based on tablet writing found in Babylonian excavations
of the 4th Millennium, B. C.*

CS: In some old *National Geographic Magazine* there was an interpretation of Babylonian hieroglyphics of this vintage, by a responsible interpreter, and it said practically the idea expressed in this poem.

CS: When I did this in 1936, it was in anticipation of automation, with its consequent unemployment and disemployment. The disemployed are unemployed, but there is a

Bilbea, I was in Babylon on Saturday night.
I saw nothing of you anywhere.
I was at the old place and the other girls were there, but
no Bilbea.

Have you gone to another house? or city?
Why don't you write?
I was sorry. I walked home half-sick.

Tell me how it goes.
Send me some kind of a letter.
And take care of yourself.

*The pestilences of the world are present and accounted for
in Sandburg's works. Man's inhumanity to man is a special
target, and Sandburg hits at it from many directions. One of
the most benign of these is the "Machine" poem, which
makes a comment on the lives of millions of workers.*

> (*Live sound effects went with this one. Merrill and Allen
> left their stools to stand flanking Miss Davis and make per-
> cussive sounds in the mechanical beat of the reading. Allen
> used two short pieces of pipe, Merrill a kitchen shredder
> and a metallic scraper to rasp against it in short, decisive
> strokes. Miss Davis, unaccompanied for the first line, used it
> to set up an emphatic rhythm in which her colleagues joined.
> After only two lines the rhythmic scheme became increas-
> ingly complicated, with certain single words like "but" and
> "all" having suddenly high values, and the repeated line "a
> man is a man and what can you do with him" being syn-
> copated in a pattern of its own. There was a diminution and
> retard over the last six lines as the machine slowed and
> stopped.*
>
> *The original poem, including two lines that were omitted
> from the stage version, appears on page 113 of the appendix.*)

The machine / yes / the machine /
Never wastes / anybody's time /
Never watches the foreman /
Never talks back /

difference between the categories because there are unemployable who are also inevitably among the unemployed.

Never says / what is right or wrong /
The machine / yes / the machine /
Cuts your production costs /
A man is a man and what can you do with him?
A man is a man and what can you do with him?
But /
A machine /
Now you take /
A machine /
No kids /
No woman /
Never hungry /
Never thirsty /
All /
A machine needs /
Is a little regular attention
And plenty /
Of grease /
And plenty /
Of grease /
And plenty /
Of grease. . . .

As you would expect, the foulest pestilence in Sandburg's file
is that scourge of our time and all previous times—War. He
agrees with Wellington that the next-most-dreadful thing to
a battle lost, is a battle won. After the end of the first World
War, Sandburg was hopeful; he wanted to believe the slogan
that it had been The War to End War. In a poem entitled
"A.E.F."—for American Expeditionary Forces—he made a
poignantly wishful image that in a sense is the quintessence
of disarmament.

There will be a rusty gun on the wall, sweetheart,
The rifle grooves curling with flakes of rust.

CS: Just a gathering up of the preposterousness of those who talk this way.

A spider will make a silver string nest in the darkest, warmest
    corner of it.
The trigger and the range-finder, they too will be rusty.
And no hands will polish the gun, and it will hang on the wall.
Forefingers and thumbs will point absently and casually
    toward it.
It will be spoken among half-forgotten, wished-to-be-forgotten
    things.
They will tell the spider: Go on, you're doing good work.

*But the gun was never on the wall long enough to rust. It
was taken down time and again, and improved. Sandburg is
no longer a wishful dreamer. He has learned through repeti-
tion—five times—that wars don't end wars but breed new
ones, each more vicious than the last. And he is impatient
with people who refuse to see that changes have been made
in war, and that mass murder will never be as restricted as in
past wars, when the dead and wounded amounted to only
twenty or thirty millions. People who are not impressed by
the changes, Sandburg considers "interesting" in the most
dismissive and cynical sense of that word.*

Interesting people who say the word "war" now as though
    the word carries the same meaning now as it did before.
Interesting people who speak of the potential war as a conflict
    wherein one comes out loser and the other a victor, and
    like in old times the loser pays the losses, the victor
    collects and everything goes on.
Interesting people who think of war and who mention war
    as though the next war could be one more war like
    other wars—
Interesting people who like to do what they have always done,
    who like to think as they have always thought, who like
    to imagine the next war can be a terrific cyclone and
    when it's over those who win the war will have a good
    time enjoying their winnings.
Interesting people. . . .

CS: I have a mild anxiety, but I don't have any worry about the next war. Fate is operating. That French marshal I quoted (in the poem) was Foch. He was a Basque, I believe.

NC: Basque? Really?

CS: Haven't you heard about the deportation of Basques from France? Seems the French put all their Basques in one exit.

Perhaps Sandburg's most crushing war poem is one he wrote not long ago, in which he carries the hard meanings of the last piece much further: It is called "The Unknown War."

Be calm, collected, easy.
In the face of the next war to come, be calm.
In the faint light and smoke of the flash and the mushroom of the first bomb blast of the Third World War, keep your wits collected.
At the information to be given out, after the few days of the fast moving next war, take it easy, be calm and collected, and say to yourself, First things come first and after this world comes another.
Beware of the matters not to be spoken of.
Beware of such matters as must be spoken of.
Watch your ears as to things heard often.
Watch your ears as to things seldom heard.
Pick and choose of what comes to your ears.
Select and sift, believe or disbelieve.
And on stated occasions, feeling a little high,
Believe perfectly in the completely unbelievable.
Thus making, under the tilt and feel of your hat,
Myths your own, miracles beheld of your eyes alone.

"Introducing," said a spieler, winking at a shill, "introducing
Miss Nuclear Fission, a wild gal in her time and she's
gonna be wilder yet, and you notice I don't dare touch
her she's that wild."
"Introducing," said a spieler with a cock-eye at a shill, "introducing Mr. Chain Reaction, her pal and dancing partner,
a hairy brute, ten billion gorillas in one and when he
tickles you, what gives? Nothin'—only you die laughin'."
So what? So we must be calm, collected, easy, facing the
next war,
And we can remember the man sitting on a red hot stove
as he sniffed the air, "Is something burning?"

Or the Kansas farmer, "We asked the cyclone to go around
our barn but it didn't hear us."

Or we can turn to the Books and take a looksee and then
take a cry or a laugh, as it pleases.

They say, do the Books: Begin your war and it becomes
something else than you saw before it began—it runs
longer or shorter than planned, it comes out like nobody
running it expected, ending with both sides saying, "We
are surprised at what happened!"

A Marshal of France spoke like a gambler flipping a card
or throwing ivory cubes, saying as though he had finished
what might be said: "The controlling factor in war is
the Unknown."

Wherefore we take a deep look into the unfathomable and
come out with a fingerhold on wriggling deductions fished
from a barrel of conniving and fructifying eels:

The bombs of the next war, if they control, hold the Unknown blasts—the bacterial spreads of the next war, if
they control, reek with the Unknown—the round-the-
curve-of-the-earth guided missiles of the next war, should
they control, will have the slide and hiss of the Unknown—
the cosmic rays or light beams carrying a moonshine kiss
of death, if and when they control, will have the mercy
of the sudden Unknown.

> We shall do the necessary.
> We shall meet the inevitable.
> We shall be prepared.
> We shall stand before the Unknown,
> aware of the controlling factor
>   the controlling factor
>   the controlling factor
>   —the Unknown.

*Perhaps there is a greater controlling factor of man's fate than
any of these . . . equally unknown, but far less morbid. A
hint of it comes in a sweet moment of* The People, Yes *when*

CS: The girl who said, "Sometime they'll give a war and nobody will come," was an adopted child of my friends, Kathryn and Lloyd Lewis. She was 8 or 9 at the time.

a little girl, watching a parade of soldiers, says: "You know something?—Sometime they'll give a war—and nobody will come. . . ."

The charming (if slender) hope of this little girl is encouraged by a song in the Songbag—a spiritual out of the Deep South, in which the study of War, known and unknown, is forever abandoned. . . .

*I'm go'n' lay down my sword and shield, I'm go'n' lay down
    my sword and shield,*
*Down by de ribber-side, down by de ribber-side, I'm go'n' lay
    down my sword and shield.*
Ain' go'n' to study war no mo'. I ain' go'n' study war no mo',
Ain' go'n' study war no mo', I ain' go'n' study war no mo'.

*I'm go'n' to wear, Lord, a starry crown, go'n' to wear a starry
    crown,*
*Down by de ribber-side, down by de ribber-side, I'm go'n' to
    wear a starry crown,*
Ain' go'n' to study war no mo'. I ain' go'n' study war no mo',
I ain' go'n' study war no mo', ain' go'n' study war no mo'.

*I'm go'n' to ride with my King, Jesus, I'm go'n' to ride with
    my King, Jesus,*
*Down by de ribber-side, down by de ribber-side, I'm go'n' to
    ride with my King, Jesus.*
Ain' go'n' study war no mo'. I ain' go'n' study war no mo',
I ain' go'n' study war no mo', I ain' go'n' study war no mo'.

I ain' go'n' study war no mo', I ain' go'n' study war no mo',
I ain' go'n' study war no mo'. . . .

The world of Sandburg has boundaries as tangible as the one we live in: it acknowledges birth as an entrance and death as an exit. Sandburg never fails to personalize death . . . sees it sometimes as a friendly Junk Man who drives his wagon

up to the houses of those who are tired of living; or as a stern Democracy who levels high and low, bringing coolness and calm to the hot and bothered; or as a nurse-mother with big arms. But at one time in Sandburg's life when he was a youth, Death was someone you might go out looking for. You might go seeking the Junk Man's wagon to hop on it. Sandburg tells about it in the Hobo chapter of Always the Young Strangers.

I had my bitter and lonely hours moving out of boy years into a grown young man. I can remember a winter when the thought came often that it might be best to step out of it all. The second thought came, "What would be the best way?" . . . I had read in detective stories how prussic acid gives death in an eyeblink, but I didn't know a doctor who would give me a prescription for it. Carbolic acid was the only poison I could think of and it would mean you wriggled and moaned with the pains and twists of dying. A revolver bullet through the head, that was clumsy to think about. To hang myself I would have to get a strong rope, find a place to fasten it, fix a box to stand on, kick the box loose, and then drop. And it might be that while strangling, my tongue would slide over my underlip and when they found me I would be too ugly a sight to think about. You have to work at several chores to hang yourself. It's more bother than it's worth. . . . I could throw myself into Lake George but I couldn't be sure that I wouldn't swim to the bank and live on. The handiest way of all, I decided, would be in front of a fast train—and the evening paper would have a headline SANDBURG BOY KILLED BY TRAIN and it would look like an accident and no disgrace to the family. After thinking about these different ways of doing away with myself, I would come out actually feeling a little cheerful. The idea came to me like a dawning, "If death is what you want, all you have to do is live on and it will come to you like a nice surprise you never imagined."

CS: Part of this poem is fact, some of it imagination. I don't want to talk about it. I just saw a certain kind of drama in it.

A woman named Elizabeth Umpstead looks back upon her life and some of the people in it, from the vantage point of her own funeral. . . .

I am Elizabeth Umpstead, dead at seventy-five years of age, and they are taking me in a polished and silver-plated box today, and an undertaker, assured of cash for his work, will supply straps to let the box down the lean dirt walls, while a quartet of singers—assured of cash for their work, sing "Nearer my God to Thee," and a clergyman, also assured of cash for his services—will pronounce the words: "Dust to dust and ashes to ashes."

I am gone from among the two-legged moving figures on top the earth now, and nobody will say my heart is someway wrong when I assert, I was the most beautiful nigger girl in northern Indiana; and men wanted my beauty, white men and black men—they wanted to take it and crush it and taste it—and I learned what they wanted and I traded on it; I schemed and haggled to get all I could for it—and so, I am one nigger girl who today has a grand funeral with all the servitors paid in spot cash.

I learned early, away back in short dresses, when a lawyer took me and used me the same as a brass cuspidor or a new horse and buggy or a swivel chair or anything that gives more life-ease for spot cash—he paid $600 cash to me for the keep of the child of my womb and his loins. And then he went to a revival, sang "Jesus Knows All About Our Troubles," moaned he was a sinner and wanted Jesus to wash his sins away. He joined the church and stood up one night before hundreds of people and blabbed to them how he used me, had a child by me, and paid me $600 cash. And I waited till one night I saw him in the public square and I slashed his face with a leather horsewhip, calling all the wild crazy names that came to my tongue to damn him and damn him and damn him, for a sneak in the face of God and man.

Well . . . they put me in a grave today, and I leave behind one child fathered by a white man lawyer, thousands of dollars in the bank, and eight houses I owned as property in the same way my mother was owned as property by white men in Tennessee.

All these I leave behind me—I, who was the most beautiful nigger girl in northern Indiana.

One of the melodies in Sandburg's bag of songs has to do with a man going around taking names—only he's not a census-taker. "The song," says Sandburg, "has an overtone of a reverie on the riddles of death, and the frail permits by which any one generation walks before the mirrors of life." It's called "Man Goin' Roun'."

There's a man goin' roun' takin' names,
There's a man goin' roun' takin' names,
An' he took my father' name
An' he leave my heart in pain,
There's a man goin' roun' takin' names.

There's a man goin' roun' takin' names,
There's a man goin' roun' takin' names,
An' he took my mother' name
An' he leave my heart in pain,
There's a man goin' roun' takin' names.

At one time when this program was being put together, we were tempted to end on the theme of death. It would be so neatly symmetrical to book a trip from the cradle to the grave. But there is too much irrepressibly alive in Sandburg to permit this. Instead we follow the contour of his own nature by making room for comic relief. For among his many other attributes, Sandburg is a collector of jokes. It doesn't matter that some of the jokes are corny, that some are old, and others

CS: I aimed at jokes and anecdotes that are common property. You remember how that "Papa Loves Mama" got in there? It wasn't in at the Portland opening. We were riding in a car after the performance—Bette, Gary, Clark Allen, you and I—and I sang the song for you. To use a Marxian phrase, you all expropriated it. *You* put it in the show; but they managed to violate my tune.

NC: How did they violate it?

CS: They got it a little too fast, and didn't get enough of a twist to the last line. I forget what it was, but there was a theory to the way *I* sang it. Yes, they butchered that song. Still, the audiences always loved it.

are goofy. They are, as Carl himself puts it, "Worth a second look." There are roughly seven varieties:

(*The movement of the three people on Sandburg's stage through the following joke section was moderately choreographic, involving many crosses, changes of character, position and attitude—to say nothing of a variety of headgear pulled on and off as occasion demanded.*

The selection of jokes kept to the etiquette of not going outside the Sandburg collection, and was obliged to end without a "topper" simply because there was no candidate for this spot in the jokebag.

To identify here which member of the company did what, went where and looked how, would only get in the way of these charming old jokes. The acting style was of course broad, the pace brisk, and the lighting—in contrast to the generally subdued and fluid scheme of most of the show— was full, bright and golden.

The classification of jokes under various titles is not part of the original Sandburg, but was added for the show. Most of these come from the pages of The People, Yes.)

COUNTRY FOLK

"How do you do, my fine friend?"
"Howdy."
"Nice looking country you have here."
"For them that likes it."
"Live here all your life?"
"Not yit."

"Which way to the post office, girl?"
"I don't know."
"You don't know much, do you?"
"No, but I ain't lost."

"Have you a criminal lawyer in this town?"
"We think so, but we haven't been able to prove it on him."

Wishes won't wash dishes.

Even God gets tired of too much hallelujah.

Love your neighbor as yourself but don't take down your fence.

THE LAST WORD
"Too bad you have to work in this kind of a soup parlor."
"I work here, but I don't eat here."

"Lieutenant, if a private calls you a damn fool, what would
    you do?"
"I'd throw him in the guard-house."
"And if he just thinks you're a damn fool and don't say it,
    what would you do?"
"Nothing."
"Well, let's let it go at that."

"That dwarf ain't worth two cents to see . . . he's six feet
    tall if he's a foot!"
"Exactly, my good lady, he's the tallest dwarf in the world!"

"Isn't that an iceberg on the horizon, Captain?"
"Yes, Madam."
"What if we get in a collision with it?"
"The iceberg, Madam, will move right along as though noth-
    ing had happened."

GOOFYISMS
I took so much medicine I was sick a long time after I got well.

You are to be hanged, and I hope it will prove a warning
    to you.

I can never get new shoes on till after I've worn 'em for a
    while.

Me? I never made a mistake in grammar but once in my life,
    and as soon as I done it, I seen it . . .

"You know who I am? I'm Marie Antoinette."
"Yesterday you said you were Cleopatra."
"Ah, but that was by another mother."

"Why on earth are you feeding doughnuts to that horse?"
"I want to see how many he eats before he asks for a cuppa
    cawfee."

"And you . . . What are you doing over there?"
"Writing a letter to myself."
"What are you telling yourself in the letter?"
"How do I know? I won't get it till tomorrow."

ERRATIC TRAINS
"You know, Bette, I think this train is running smoother
    now."
"Yes, . . . it's off the track now."

SHORT NOVELS
Papa loved Mama
Mama loved men
Mama's in the graveyard
Papa's in the pen.

WOMEN THROUGH THE AGES
"Say, Bette told me that you told her the secret I told you
    not to tell her."
"I told her not to tell you I told her."
"Well, don't tell her I told you she told me."

"Miss Bette, as you look back over your 99 years, what gives
    you the greatest satisfaction?"
"Young man, you can tell your readers the greatest satisfaction
    is that I haven't got an enemy in the world."
"That's a beautiful thought—not an enemy in the world!"
"Yes sir, I outlived 'em all."

"I am John Jones."

"Take a chair."

"Yes, I am John Throckmorton Jones."

"Is that possible? Take two chairs."

"Get off this estate!"

"What for?"

"Because it's mine."

"Where did you get it?"

"From my father."

"Where did he get it?"

"From his father."

"And where did he get it?"

"He fought for it."

"Well, I'll fight you for it."

> (*Miss Davis broke off the Joke section with a caudal "End of comic relief!" To everyone's mild surprise, it got a laugh on its own.*)

Sandburg's biography of Abraham Lincoln is easily the Everest of his personal range. The work runs to a million-and-a-half words . . . and we close tonight with a few of them from the final pages of The Prairie Years.

> (*The introduction actually ran longer than this, by way of preparing for the mood and substance of a song entitled "A Hundred Years Ago," which Allen sang and hummed behind Miss Davis' opening words about Lincoln, and which he also reprised at the end. Since the effect depended entirely on sound, light and atmosphere, and cannot be conveyed on the printed page, it is left out here.*
>
> *Within Miss Davis' narration, Merrill portrayed Lincoln and spoke his fragments of dialogue. For Lincoln's farewell speech, he crossed up to the dais supporting the throne-chair and used it as the back platform of the train. He made his speech, then sat down gravely as Miss Davis concluded. Lights faded on both of the Merrills as Allen sang, "A hundred years is a very long time, oh, yes, oh . . ."*)

NC: How long did you work on your Lincoln?

CS: Twelve years of active work on *The War Years*. I finished it in '39; then came proofreading, the writing of an introduction and the captioning of some 400 halftones and some 250 or more zinc cuts. Of course before that there was the work on *The Prairie Years*.

NC: How long did *that* take?

CS: About five years. Preceding that, I read basic Lincoln material over the course of 30 years. That would bring me back almost to my college days, when the Ida Tarbell series [on Lincoln] ran in *McClure's Magazine*.

NC: Were any scraps left over when you put down the final period in the manuscript?

CS: From time to time across the years of writing, there would be things that didn't fit into a chapter, and I had a repository called WEAVE. When I was making a final revision, I went through all of those notes. I didn't use any of them, but I may yet do a book with those notes.

NC: When you realized you were finally finished after such a very long haul, what were your feelings?

CS: Let me tell you first how I felt while I was *still* working at it. At times I used to get terrible headaches—prongs of pain across my head— sometimes I thought I might be getting set for a brain hemorrhage. And I had a prayer across that time, like some old bird in the Old Testament: "Lord, if Thou wilst permit me to finish this task, then Thou mayst have me."

NC: Did these head pains disappear after you shipped off the manuscript?

CS: Yes, as I moved into a new regime.

NC: Did you miss Lincoln after spending so much time with him?

CS: It was like leaving an old friend. In my imagination I had been living with him. He was

Lincoln was fifty-one years old. With each year since he had become a grown man, his name and ways, and stories about him, had been spreading among plain people and their children. So tall and so bony, with so peculiar a slouch and so easy a saunter; so sad and so haunted-looking, so quizzical and comic, as if hiding a lantern that lighted and went out and that he lighted again.

Like something out of a picture book for children, he was. His form of slumping arches and his face of gaunt sockets were a shape a Great Artist had scrawled from careless clay.

He didn't wear clothes. Rather clothes hung upon him as if on a rack to dry, or on a loose ladder up a windswept chimney. His clothes, to keep the chill or the sun off, seemed to whisper, "He put us on when he was thinking about something else."

The year of the big debates a boy had called out, "There goes old Mr. Lincoln," and Lincoln, hearing it, remarked to a friend: "They commenced calling me old when I was scarcely thirty." Often when people called him "Old Abe" they meant he had the texture and quaint friendliness of old hand-made Bibles, old calfskin law books, or wagon axles always willing in storm or stars.

A girl skipping along a sidewalk stumbled on a brick and fell backwards, just as Lincoln came along. He caught her, lifted her up in his arms, put her gently down and asked: "What is your name?"

"Mary Tufts."

"Well, Mary, when you reach home, tell your mother you have rested in Abraham's bosom."

Mr. Lincoln liked to tell of a strict judge: "He would hang a man for blowing his nose in the street, but he would quash the indictment if it failed to specify which hand he blew it with."

On being told of a certain man saying, "I can't understand those speeches of Lincoln," he laughed, "There are always some fleas a dog can't reach."

A lawyer was talking business to Lincoln once, at home, and suddenly the door opened. Mrs. Lincoln put her head in

a habit. But there were no tears on parting. Those had come earlier. As I put it at Gettysburg [note: just the night before this conversation, Sandburg had been telecast nationally in the remarkable *Sandburg at Gettysburg* documentary program], I found, as I was writing the chapter where Lincoln meets death, that I could not see the copy paper in the typewriter, for the tears. In the next chapter, called "A Tree is Best Measured When it's Down," I managed to have dry eyes; but in the last chapter of all, about the funeral train, I wept along with the American people.

NC: I was very much moved by the chapter called "The Pardoner." Tears, I mean.

CS: Yes, a deeply moving chapter.

NC: What a man!

CS: Mark Van Doren says that Lincoln was the most interesting man that ever lived. Every once in a while I meet a man who says, "Lincoln was the *greatest* man that ever lived."

and snapped the question whether he had done an errand she told him to do. He looked up quietly, said he had been busy, but would attend to it as soon as he could. Mrs. Lincoln wailed; she was neglected, abused, insulted . . . The door slammed and she was gone. The visiting lawyer muttered his surprise. Lincoln laughed: "Why, if you knew how much good that little eruption did, what a relief it was to her, and if you knew her as well as I do, you would be glad she had had an opportunity to explode."

A cold drizzle of rain was falling one February 11, when Lincoln and his party of fifteen were to leave Springfield on the eight o'clock at the Great Western Railway station. Chilly gray mist hung the circle of the prairie horizon. A short locomotive stood puffing with a baggage car and special passenger car coupled on. A thousand people crowded in and around the brick station, inside of which Lincoln was standing, and one by one came hundreds of old friends, wishing him luck and God-speed, all faces solemn.

A path was made for Lincoln from the station to his car; hands stretched out for one last handshake. He hadn't intended to make a speech; but on the platform of the car, as he turned and saw his home people, he took off his hat, stood perfectly still, and raised a hand for silence . . .

"My friends—No one, not in my situation, can appreciate my feeling of sadness at this parting. To this place, and the kindness of these people, I owe everything. Here I have lived a quarter of a century, and have passed from a young to an old man. Here my children have been born, and one is buried. I now leave, not knowing when, or whether ever, I may return . . . Trusting in [God,] who can go with me, and remain with you and be every where for good, let us confidently hope that all will yet be well. To His care commending you, as I hope in your prayers you will commend me, I bid you an affectionate farewell."

Bells rang, there was a grinding of wheels, the train moved and carried Lincoln away from his home-town and folks. The tears were not yet dry on some faces when the train had faded into the gray to the east.

SANDBURG TRIBUTE AT U.C.L.A.

THE TRIBUTE was held in Royce Hall, University of California at Los Angeles, on the evening of November 23, 1958.

Dr. Frank Baxter was master of ceremonies. In the course of the program, the following actors and actresses (listed alphabetically, not in order of appearance) performed selections from Sandburg's writings:

James Backus   *Slabs of the Sunburnt West* (Section 5)
Vanessa Brown   *Boxes and Bags*
Raymond Burr   *Work Gangs*
Francis X. Bushman   *Last Answers*
Jeff Chandler   *Man the Moon Shooter*
Hans Conreid   *On a Flimmering Floom You Shall Ride*
Paul Douglas   *Old Timers*
Glenn Ford   *A Father Sees a Son Nearing Manhood* (Section 9, The People, Yes)
Coleen Gray   *Fog*
Juan Hernandez   *Monkey of Stars*
Jeff Hunter   *Buffalo Bill*
Martha Hyer   *The Breathing of the Earth* (Section 92, The People, Yes)

Burt Lancaster *Brancusi*

Jack Lemmon *The People Learn, Unlearn, Learn* (Section 97, *The People, Yes*)

Lisa Lu *The Fishes Though Deep in the Water* (Section 67, *The People, Yes*)

Margo *Joy*

Paddy McCormick *We Must Be Polite*

Hugh O'Brian *Chicago*

Anthony Quinn *Threes*

Eva Marie Saint *Explanations of Love*

Frank Silvera *Jazz Fantasia*

Jan Sterling *Very, Very Important*

Others who participated but did not read Sandburg poems were: Ray Bradbury, writer; Joe Hyams, columnist; Tom Pryor, then New York *Times* Hollywood correspondent; William Stout, radio commentator. The choir of the Hollywood First Methodist Church, under the direction of Dr. Norman Söreng Wright, sang a musical setting of "Buffalo Bill" composed expressly for the occasion by Irving Gertz.

A film episode of an interview with Sandburg on his farm at Flat Rock, North Carolina, was contributed by the interviewer, Edward R. Murrow. And of course Sandburg himself appeared.

Concept, script and direction of the program were by Norman Corwin; production by Leonard Karzmar.

Tape recordings of the Tribute were deposited in the archives of the Sandburg Room at the University of Illinois, and the Theater Arts Department of U.C.L.A.

NOTES ON DIRECTION

THOUGH THESE classify as shop talk to the lay reader, they may be of possible interest to those wishing a sort of stereo-view of the material discussed. In a theatrical presentation, one simply cannot "read" material as though going over proofs, or putting something into a court record. On the other hand, it is important to avoid the quality of a "recitation"—dread word!—and yet there is the danger of going overboard, as they say in the trade . . . on either side of the boat.

These notes were by no means all that was said on the subject of each poem; one has to live with a piece, fuss with it, quarrel with it, reach for things the author himself may never have suspected were coiled up inside. The medium of a live audience is many worlds removed from the printed page when it comes to material not originally conceived for the stage. Just as one did not expect a mild laugh on the reference to Mildred Klinghofer's third and fourth husbands, as noted in the Introduction to this volume, neither did one expect an explosive laugh on "If you hate a man let him live. You may live to see him suffer." Unfailingly, in seventy different cities, audiences rocked with laughter when Merrill or Sullivan or Erickson came to it. One laugh was disruptive, the other welcome.

There were of course many laughs in the show, along with the sober and even frightening moments. But no one expected that everything would stop while audiences laughed in a series of great breaking waves at two moments; first, when Miss Davis, as a Solomonic Hongdorsh, advises against telling a frozen fish it is a hot waffle; then, in the rapturous "Meditations on the Forms of Love," at the point where Miss Davis, expanding on the size of elephantine love, cries out: "Jesus, he's big!" At times in certain theaters the laughs here had the suddenness and impact of a sonic boom. The reader may not even crack a smile at those points. What then makes the difference? First, the magic of contagion in an audience. The threshold of humor, or at least of what seems funny, varies with the size of an audience as well as with its character. While a living room full of people might loudly enjoy these two points, the effect could never approach the storm of laughter in a full theater.

But even more important is the way the line or the phrase is "performed"—a term that must aseptically be substituted for "read" because of the unfortunate connotations of the latter. Miss Davis framed the frozen fish passage by resting her hands on the sides of her lectern and leaning forward as though to communicate a cosmic truth to an audience throbbing for enlightenment, then speaking the line with admonitory urgence, like an Old Testament prophet scolding the younger generation for backsliding among idols. In the case of "Jesus, he's big!"—(never misconstrued as an irreverence, I am happy to say)—it came so suddenly, unexpectedly and with such force, that the audience was caught by surprise and laughed as much at its own surprise as at the humor of this backstreet superlative coming in the middle of something essentially lyrical.

But the whole program, from the standpoint of the actors

and myself as director, was studded with curiosities, anomalies, and surprises. Miss Davis, whose career has encompassed a wider range of materials than that of most first-magnitude stars, said she had never undertaken anything faintly resembling *The World of Carl Sandburg* in terms of the unique challenges it presented.

The following notes, addressed to Barry Sullivan, were partial and transitory, but they will serve to indicate something of the rationale and approach that made up a sort of supply line to each item of Sandburg.

INTRODUCTION
Keep a balance between the too-formal and excessively in-
formal. The first would scare people into thinking they are
in for something awfully long-hair; the second would promise
less dignity than the name of Sandburg connotes.

BROTHER NOTHINGS
Grave at first, then increasingly boastful and peremptory in
your insistence on the way other Nothings must greet you
when you come to them—with the ultimate demand that
they *KISS* you, topping the rest. "Greet, hold, shake" are
sharp demands too, but "KISS" is the crowning one.

DESTA PODESTA LULLABY
You have two seconal pills and a tranquilizer inside you before
you start. Close your eyes on the first line, "Come to me
dreaminess," and invoke sleep, sweet sleep. Fight a tendency
to monotony, which the lulling nature of the piece tempts
one into. "Sleep, slip, slag" and "springerly, sprangerly,
sprong" are alliterative and sibilant, like a nestful of lazy

snakes or a steam radiator half-heartedly hissing under low pressure. Do not drop the last two lines in a bucket. Let's hear the last words of each sentence—especially "slow" and "moon," which end lines twice each. The last line is almost never audible out in row D. Quiet, yes, but not gone.

ADVICE TO A SON

This and the next piece are the first really solid serious works of the show . . . a major change of spirit and pace, showing us Sandburg as a man of wisdom.

Go into the father piece with a distinct attitude, different from anything you have done on the show up to then. It is no trifling thing to advise a son on how to meet life. Few are equipped to do it well, and Sandburg is one of the few. Never be easy or casual—your audience is hungry for mature advice; don't rush them from thought to thought. Believe in it before you say the first line, and take each subject (being hard; being soft; a tough will; desire; money; being a fool; being alone; being different; being lazy; seeking deep) as separate but related concepts. Sell each of them a little—not obviously, but with the earnestness that attaches to everything one passes along as counsel to a good friend, or someone soliciting advice. End with a slight retard.

COLORADO GRAVEYARD

In this, as in other basically serious pieces that have some wry lines in them, the attitude is no different from what other serious pieces require—we must not *ourselves* think it funny, but let the audience draw what fun it likes from the lines. The same exact key is in Bette's following poem—"The law says you and I belong to each other, George." . . . and she does this with a crisp sardonicism. You too are sardonic in this one, as you contemplate those two idiots who shot it out over a piece of real estate. It must never lose its sense of detachment—the detachment of an observer and commentator rather than a participant.

CARELESS LOVE

The last moments of your chorus have generally been off-key, giving the effect of running the whole number down hill. If on further rehearsal of this song with Clark, and further performances, the melody remains too tricky to handle with safety, I would suggest that the number end with Bette's chorus. If, on the other hand, it yields to further efforts, then I would suggest that you continue to sing the opening lines just as brashly and broadly as you are now doing, but insinuate in the performance a degree of cynicism and an attitude of "to Hell with it all," as justified by the lines. Your money is spent and gone and the girl you love doesn't give a damn about your being broke. In fact, she passes your door a-singing a song. You are not really *gay* about this at all—only drunkenly bitter—hence the rowdy attitude. Loud, but sardonic.

GLASS

Not too fast; not too big. Make it tart and dry, like a Martini.

NEWSPAPERS

This too must be dry, even a little sardonic from the very beginning. You do not love newspapers but distrust them— they are good for building fires, wrapping bundles, sitting on at picnics, and throwing away. The fact that the piece involves stage movement, does not mean it needs to be jouncy or airy. A too-boyish quality in this makes the performer a newsboy rather than a shrewd, ironic observer. Do not *relish* passing out the papers to Clark and Bette, do not *delight* in the picnic.—You have been dragged to it by your wife and it's hot and the beer is warm. As for "newspapers telling beforehand what is going to happen after—" the "maybe" is the topper; in other words, Sandburg does not have high respect for the prognosticators of the press—they are too often full of wind. The only time in this piece that Carl is at all kind to the press is when he qualifies the "terrible"—by allowing, "when terrible things happen." We don't want to lose the energy of this piece, but should consider it a series of factual demonstrations, tinged with irony, rather than a good time to be had by all.

SLIPHORN JAZZ

You're a wise guy—you know the answers—you hang around pool rooms; you play the races; you like women and have messed around with them; you were deliriously happy with one of them, in fact *too* happy—and when it busted up so did you. Busted *hard*—real *hard*—and it took a hell of a while to put yourself together again. You've never forgotten the experience. You vowed never to let yourself get too *damn* happy—too *happy*-happy—because it's those *happy*-happy people who bust *hard* when they do bust.

The man you are counseling is a good Joe—you like him— you don't want to see him get hurt. It's okay for him to be crazy for a broad, but you tip him not to go too far. You got up from the canvas after your woman floored you, and you're now reasonably cheerful and flip but the advice you are giving out is sound underneath the chirpy jaunt.

HATE

Never ride over the laugh after "you may live to see him suffer." Let it sink in; let the laughter almost die before you follow up. And never a smile throughout. This was not *meant* to produce a big laugh. That the audience laughs and loves it is their affair—and we are glad of it—but basically this is a coolly philosophic piece, like the Colorado Graveyard. Retard the end always.

TELL ME YOU LOVE ME

Be passionate, irked, frustrated, explosive. This comes out of you under great pressure and distress. The bitch has been so cold to you, and you have loved her madly, so madly you want to hear her say she loves you, she cares, even if she has to lie when she says it.

You will kill this piece dead if you hurry it or sound less

than utterly despairing and frustrated. The cross upstage must be vital and urgent. You must *burn* with all these conflicting passions—you'd slug her if you didn't worship every corpuscle in her. You are too civilized to beat her, too helpless to cut loose from her, and not proud enough to avoid abasing yourself. It is the abasement of a man pleading almost for his life, since he cannot live without her love. And he's not getting it.

Don't be tame as you stand beside her. Abject, pleading, vexed, ashamed, debased, hopelessly in the grip of your obsession.

MOTHER FACES
What will your own little daughter become? A ballerina, a schoolteacher, a nurse, actress, doctor, housewife, acrobat? Mothers, usually even more than fathers, wonder beforehand what comes after, what will happen to their kids. In this one, put yourself in the place of these wondering, hopeful women. None wants her child to be a criminal, a monster, a failure, a despot, an assassin. Sympathy is the core of this piece—sympathy and understanding for those mothers who know that love is a deep well—so deep no man has ever plumbed the bottom of it.—Let us feel the warmth, the understanding and sympathy for the special love of mothers.

AUDIENCES
This can use a factual approach, as though coming out of long observation of the behavior of audiences. In a way this is related to the section on Glass, Tablecloths, Newspapers, Fingers, etc. If the audience is a good one, the "quick as greased lightning" allusion should be tactfully underscored; if the shoe fits some less flattering definition, take care that the reading at this point doesn't become too personal, otherwise the audience will feel guilty and sheepish and even resentful.

THE UNKNOWN WAR
Be careful not to drop the word "war" in the title. Curiously, you do that in another moment of your narration in which

you are introducing one of Bette's war pieces. War is terrible, all right, but not so terrible that we should not speak the word loudly.

Once or twice there has been a chuckle in the second spieler line. There should be no lightness at all in this relentless piece. The audience can be trusted to laugh at the line of the man sitting on the stove and the Kansas farmer, but it must not seem to you funny, only ironic—and the laugh itself is not one of good humor, but an uneasy laugh.

LINCOLN

There was always something tired about the grown Lincoln. He moved slowly, like a giraffe, and except when excited, his speech, even in ordinary conversation, was ambling. Sad, tired, with a quiet though incisive humor—this is the key to the interpolations in the first part. Split the difference between facing Bette and facing the audience in this area—a 45 degree angle toward Stage Right.

In the farewell speech, tinge the words with a feeling about the *occasion*—it is a farewell, perhaps forever (it *was* forever), to his home town and the people, the friends he knew and loved there. What should have been a hero's glorious send-off was made solemn by the tragedy of imminent war, and the grave responsibilities attached to the presidency. Lincoln is touched by the turnout of his friends, touched by memories of his life here, the rearing of his family, the death of a son. As most thoughtful men do when they go on a journey, or into a battle from which they may not emerge alive, he calls upon God to grace the occasion, and go both with him and his listeners.

GENERAL NOTES

The productional effect most desirable in this show is one of a smooth blending of elements, and a kind of easy lyrical segue from one to the other. This is the dominant scheme of the lighting and the arrangement of the material. An angular or obtrusive effect such as loudly flipping a page, or a listening posture that calls attention to itself, tends to break the rhythm in a subtle and cumulative way. While there are things to be commended about the way you now open "Be proud if you want to," your long silence and the business of watching Bette while she crosses to the upstage throne constitute a change in rhythm. At all times, when anyone crosses upstage *in narration* no attention is paid to the cross by others on the stage; the object of this is to mask these movements as much as possible; to keep the attention of the audience focused on what is being said rather than to detract from this by watching a piece of movement.

Though much emphasis was placed in early rehearsals on the required sobriety of the over-all picture, we naturally do not want a stern or remote attitude to supersede the geniality and warmth which has been present in your performance. It is a question of distributing proportions in just the right amounts.

ORIGINAL "MACHINE" LINES

The machine yes the machine
never wastes anybody's time
never watches the foreman
never talks back
never talks what is right or wrong
never listens to others talking or if
    it does listen it doesn't hear
never says we've been thinking, or, our
    feeling is like this
the machine yes the machine cuts your production cost
a man is a man and what can you do with him?
but a machine now you take a machine
no kids no woman never hungry never thirsty
all a machine needs is a little regular attention and plenty
    of grease.